Baby Animals

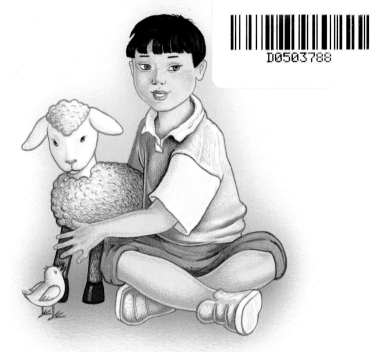

by Margie Sigman
illustrated by Valerie Sokolova

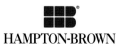

HAMPTON-BROWN

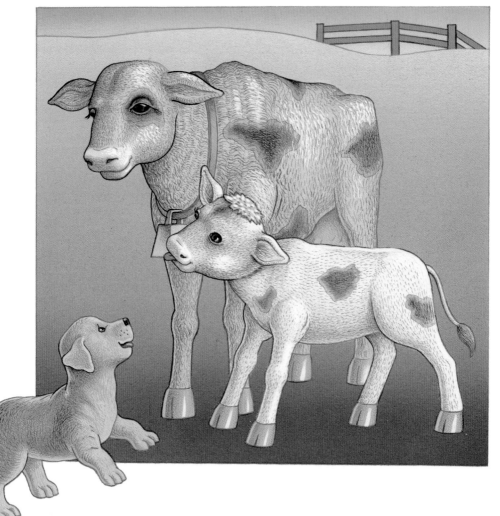

I like your calf.

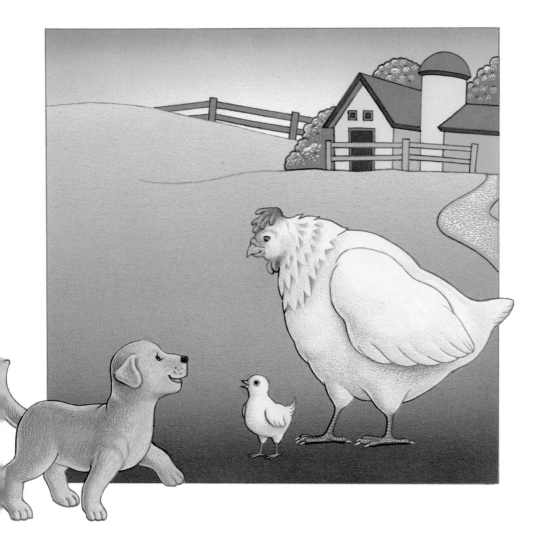

I like your chick.

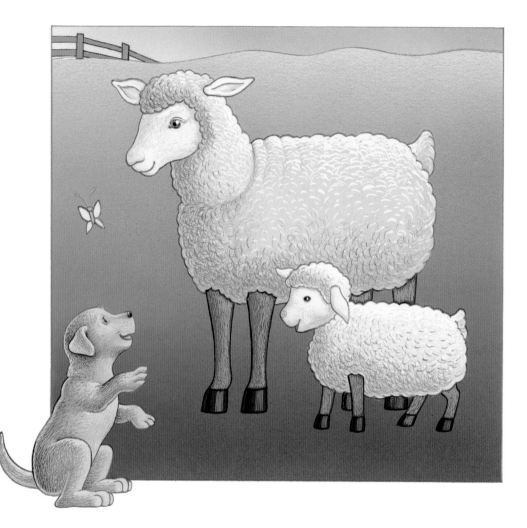

I like your lamb.

4

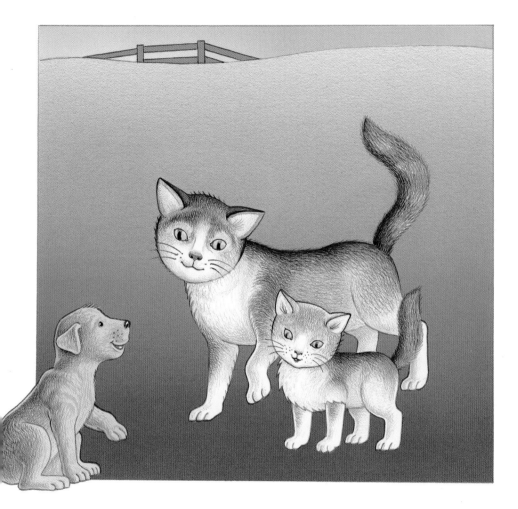

I like your kitten.

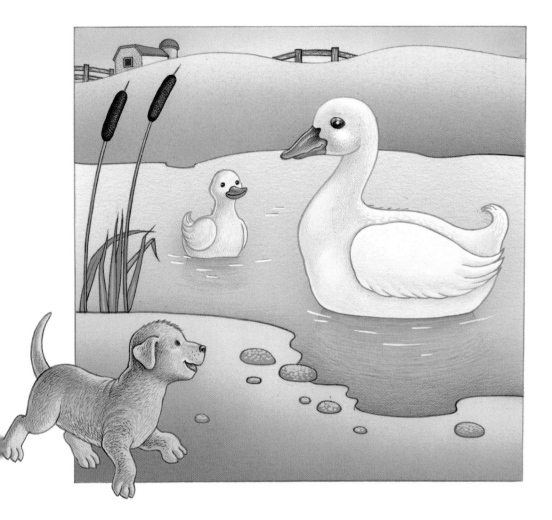

I like your duckling.

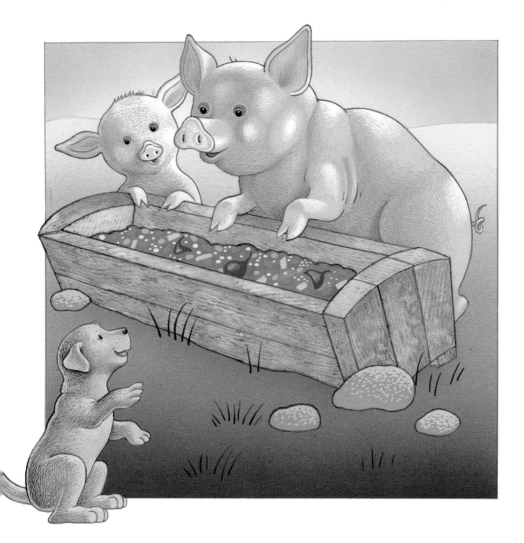

I like your piglet.

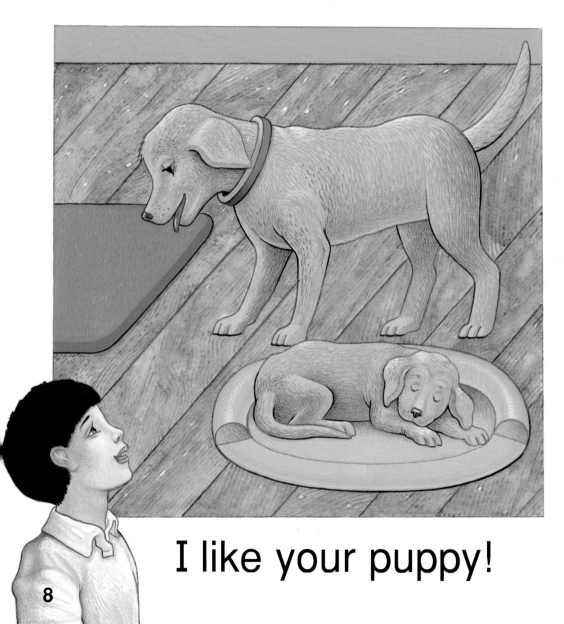

I like your puppy!